PIER RAILWAYS AND TRAMWAYS

MARTIN EASDOWN

AMBERLEY

Harwich Train Ferry
During the First World War, train ferry berths were established at Richborough and Southampton to ship war materials over to the Western Front. Following their wartime use, the linkspans and other equipment were relocated to Harwich where a goods only train ferry service ran to Zeebrugge in Belgium between 1924 and 1987. The berth at Harwich was reached by a wooden pier, pictured here just after the Second World War. Other train ferry services in the United Kingdom were located at: Granton to Burntisland, 1844–90 (replaced by a bridge), Broughty Ferry to Tayport, 1848–87 (replaced by a bridge), Langstone to Bembridge, 1885–88, Southampton, 1918–20, Richborough, 1918–23 (both constructed for wartime traffic to the Continent), and Immingham, 1922–23; and Dover to Dunkerque, 1936–95.

For Tom, a railway man

First published 2025

Amberley Publishing
The Hill, Stroud
Gloucestershire, GL5 4EP

www.amberley-books.com

ISBN 978 1 3981 2407 3 (print)
ISBN 978 1 3981 2408 0 (ebook)

British Library Cataloguing in Publication Data.
A catalogue record for this book is available from the British Library.

Typesetting by SJmagic DESIGN SERVICES, India.
Printed in Great Britain.

Appointed GPSR EU Representative:
Easy Access System Europe Oü, 16879218
Address: Mustamäe tee 50, 10621, Tallinn, Estonia
Contact Details: gpsr.requests@easproject.com, +358 40 500 3575

Contents

Swanage (Old)

The provision of a pier and tramway at Swanage was proposed as a means of exporting Purbeck stone from nearby quarries, and the pier, which consisted of a 240-foot causeway leading to 550-foot timber pier, was opened in February 1860. However, local opposition to the tramway meant that only 375 yards of it was built along the pier and promenade to the bankers of cut stone awaiting shipment. The tramway, which was horse-drawn, originally sported a standard gauge of 4 feet 8½ inches, but it was regauged to 2 feet 6 inches in the 1890s. Two cranes were provided on the pier to assist in the loading and unloading of goods. The handling of freight continued on the pier after the opening of the adjoining steamer pier in 1896, but the old pier was eventually left to decay and today only some of the piles remain standing. A 330-foot section of the tramway remains imbedded in the promenade.

Above: **Rhos-on-Sea**

Here are two examples of railways/tramways used in the construction of piers that were not retained after they were fully opened. This is the pier at Rhos-on-Sea in North Wales under construction in 1894 and a wooden track can be seen, which was probably used to propel a crane along the pier. The 1,400-foot-long pier was opened on 11 April 1895 for use principally as a landing stage for steamers, but was demolished in 1954.

Below: **Brighton Palace**

Work commenced on building Brighton's Palace Pier on 7 November 1891, but financial difficulties meant that the first part of the pier was not opened until 20 May 1899. During its construction, a 3-foot 6-inch-gauge tramway was laid to assist with the works (pictured here *c.* 1900) and although permission was granted to convert it to passenger carrying, it was not retained upon the full opening of the 1,760-foot-long pier on 3 April 1901.

Introduction

The seaside pier is a well-loved landmark around the coast of the United Kingdom and it was an integral part of the development of the great British seaside, which reached its zenith in the late Victorian and Edwardian periods. From their origins as landing stages for boats, piers blossomed into fashionable marine promenades over the sea, complete with pavilions and amusements of all kinds.

Prior to the coming of the railway from the 1830s, and thereafter in tandem with it, visitors often arrived at the resorts by sea – initially by hoys and then paddle steamers. The earliest piers, at Ryde (1814), Brighton (1823), Southend-on-Sea (1830), Walton-on-the-Naze (1830), and Herne Bay (1832) – were built as landing stages, although the Chain Pier at Brighton, in particular, soon became a popular promenade, for which customers were prepared to pay a handsome toll. Nevertheless, pier development initially remained sparse and those early wooden piers were prone to attacks by marine worms. However, it was the building of the two iron piers at Margate (1855) and Southport (1860) that was to prove to be the template for pier design during their boom period over the next fifty years. This explosion of pier building was assisted by the passing of the Piers and Harbours Act in 1861, which eased parliamentary assent for their construction, and piers began sprouting up in coastal towns big and small.

To save the legs and aching arms of passengers, the longer piers often boasted railways and tramways to carry them and their baggage from the shore to the steamers at the pier head, whilst other piers had simple baggage tramways that were often originally used to assist in the construction of the pier. Although the terms 'railway' and 'tramway' have often been confusingly used as regards to pier lines (such as at Southend-on-Sea and Southport), a 'railway' was laid directly onto the decking and was fenced off from the promenade section whilst a 'tramway' was laid flush with the decking and could sometimes be walked upon. Various methods of propulsion were used. The rolling stock on the early piers was usually hand-propelled, horse-drawn, cable-operated, or sail-driven. Later, electric third rails, petrol and diesel locomotives, steam engines, and battery cars were used. They ran on a variety of track gauges. There was even an electric railway that ran through the sea between piers at Brighton and Rottingdean – the extraordinary 'Daddy-long-legs' railway.

Unlike previous books on pier railways and tramways, I have not limited myself to just including self-contained pier passenger lines that commenced at the beginning of the pier and ended at the sea end, but have encompassed piers that had railways connected to the national network. These had fully fledged stations, and although those that ran onto harbour walls and served ferry traffic, such as at Dover Admiralty (1864), Weymouth (1865), and Folkestone (1876), have been well-documented, there were also long-lost lines on more traditional-looking wooden piled piers such as at Piel (1846), New Passage (1863), and Portskewett (1864) that are less well-known. Several pier stations were actually located near the pier rather than on it and I have also embraced examples of these. Miniature railways used to transport people up and down the pier purely for pleasure are also included, although as most of these were a short-lived attraction during the 1940s and 1950s, historical records of them can be sparse. However, I have not been able to include military and industrial piers that had railways and tramways (including Fairlie NATO, Fort Victoria, Haslar Royal Naval Hospital (Gosport), Portland Roads, Shoeburyness, and Spurn Head, and Welsh industrial jetties such as Llanddulas, Trefor, and Penmaenmawr), although there are postcard views of Morecambe

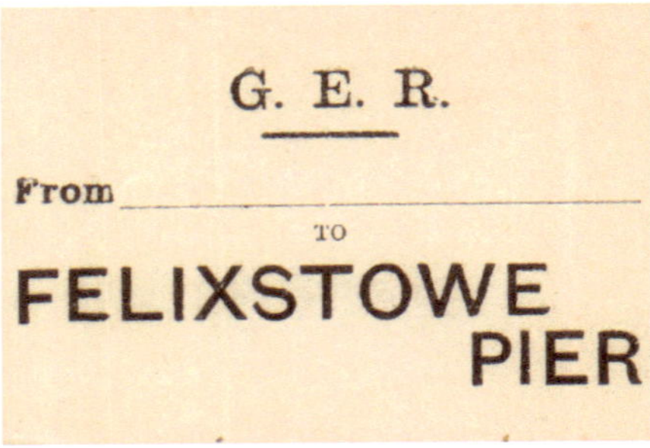

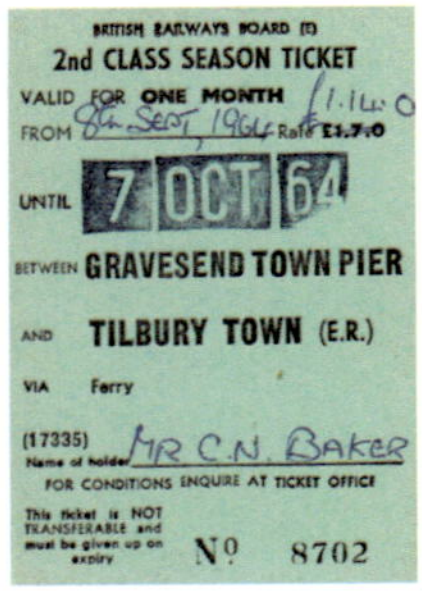

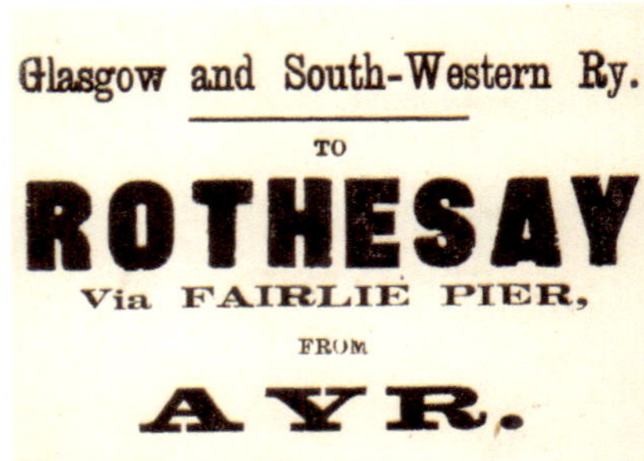

Stone Jetty and Ballyvoy, Fairhead, at the end of the book. Also missing are the rail-connected Trinty House piers at Burton Ferry and Harwich. I have included the railway piers that are now in the Republic of Ireland, but which at the time of their construction were in the United Kingdom, except the small goods-only piers at Baltimore, Cappagh, Courtmacsherry, Fahan, Fenit, and Rathmullen (although Schull has been included as an example of this type).

Herne Bay can claim to have had the earliest pier railway/tramway when a sail-driven vessel named *Old Neptune's Car* was in use from 1833 to ferry people along the 3,633-foot-long pier. There was even an experiment to run an atmospheric railway along the pier in 1845. The 1840s also saw a sail and manual-propelled tramway installed on the pier at Southend-on-Sea (1846), which had just become the longest in Britain at 1¼ miles, and railway piers at Piel (1846) and New Holland (1848). The gateway to the Isle of Wight, Ryde Pier, acquired a tramway pier in 1864 and a railway one, connected to the Isle of Wight Railway, in 1880. On the other side of the Solent, a pier to compete with the existing crossing to Ryde was opened at Stokes Bay in 1863, and the Landport & Southsea Tramway began running onto the Clarence Pier in 1865. The 1860s also saw Southport Pier, which vied with Herne Bay as the second longest pleasure pier in the country, open a cable-operated tramway in 1864, and the ferry crossing of the River Severn between England and Wales used two railway piers at New Passage and Portskewett. Fierce competitors, the South Eastern Railway and the London, Chatham & Dover Railway opened railway piers on the Medway Estuary at Queenborough (1876) and Port Victoria (1882) to compete for Continental boat traffic. Wemyss Bay (1863) was one of a number of railway piers in Scotland that served the steamer traffic on the Clyde, and there were others that handled the loch steamers.

Electricity became the favoured propulsion for the pier self-contained lines after Southend built its new 1⅓-mile-long iron pier and electric railway in 1889–90. Other long piers at Herne Bay, Walton-on-the-Naze, Felixstowe and Southport all acquired electric railways/tramways between 1899 and 1905. The pier that served the Hythe–Southampton Ferry gained its charming little electric railway in 1922 that still trundles along it today little altered. Elsewhere though, many pier railways and tramways have gone, victims of both the decline in pier numbers and the shrinkage of the railway network. Aside from Hythe, the only surviving pier self-contained railway is the famous one at Southend-on-Sea, which has recently acquired new trains. The piers at Ryde, Lymington, and Wemyss Bay remain connected to the national network, as do the harbour piers in Scotland at Ardrossan, Gourock, and Stranraer.

The author thanks Linda Sage, Phil Johnson, and Peter Scott for their assistance with this book. Original documents from national and county archives have been used as source material along with newspaper reports and publications on piers and railways. Space precludes giving a fuller history of the piers featured in this book, and the railways that served them, but there are other publications available (including the author's own pier books) which provide this detail. I hope you will enjoy this first book to give an overall pictorial history of the railways and tramways that served the piers of the British Isles.

Martin Easdown

Self-Contained Pier Railways and Tramways

South Shields

The three harbour breakwater piers at Tynemouth, South Shields, and Roker in the north-east of England were not pier railways in the conventional sense, but they each sported rail tracks to propel the huge cranes that had been used to build the piers and were kept to assist in their maintenance. This postcard from 1903 shows the track on South Shields Pier with the crane at the sea end. In the background the pier at Tynemouth was undergoing reconstruction following storm damage in 1897. The two piers were completed and opened in 1895 to a length of 2,950 feet at Tynemouth and 5,170 feet at South Shields. The pier at Roker was opened on 23 September 1903 to a length of 2,800 feet, and its large crane on rails, known as 'Goliath', was driven by gas engines supplied by pipes running in a tunnel underneath the pier. The tunnel is open to the public, and the rail tracks are still in situ.

Above: **Bangor**
Striding out into the Menai Straits, the pier at Bangor is one of the most attractive of British seaside piers and it was opened on 14 May 1896 to a length of 1,500 feet. A tramway used in its construction was retained to carry the baggage of passengers using the steamers, but this was removed in 1921 following repairs to the pier after 150 feet of it had been damaged in December 1914 by the cargo vessel *Christiania*.

Below: **Beaumaris**
The pier at Beaumaris on Anglesey was opened on 1 May 1846 to a length of 563 feet and was constructed partly of solid masonry infilled with rubble and partly of wood. Improvements to the pier were carried out in 1895, which included the laying of a 2-foot 6-inch narrow-gauge tramway to convey baggage to and from the steamers. This fell into disrepair during the First World War, although some of the rails can still be seen.

Blackpool North

Above is an early view of Blackpool North Pier, *c.* 1870, showing the tramway track used in its construction boarded over. The pier was designed by the great pier builder Eugenius Birch and was constructed by Robert Laidlaw and Sons of Glasgow. The tramway was not retained after the pier was opened on 21 May 1863. In the year 1991 a tramway returned to the pier (seen below at the Theatre stop) when an 824-foot-long, 3-foot-gauge line was opened on 2 September. The tram car was built by Harry Steer Engineering of Breaston in Derbyshire and it consisted of a three-car unit constructed with a galvanised steel chassis and colour impregnated fibreglass exterior cladding. The cars were totally enclosed and had a passenger capacity of fifty-six people, with an equal number of seated and standing passengers, who initially paid 50p for a ride. The photograph shows the tram in 1998.

Blackpool North

The 1991 tram on Blackpool North Pier (seen above at the shore end station) was one-man operated and powered at a sedate 5 mph by a Perkins 2.3-litre, three-cylinder diesel engine mounted in the centre car. This drove a Linde variable displacement pump supplying power to the eight-wheel mounted motors and de-energising the eight fail-safe brakes. There were four powered wheels on the centre car and two powered and four braked wheels on each of the driving cars. As the pier was not particularly long, the tram only took three minutes to complete one journey, and most people preferred to walk along it. The tramway received covered stops, but by 2004 it had ceased running. A land train now runs down the pier during the high season and the photograph below shows it at the former tram stop at the shore end of the pier in June 2018.

Bognor Regis

The pier at Bognor Regis was constructed by J. E. Dowson at a cost of £5,500 to the design of Joseph William Wilson and was officially opened on 4 May 1865. It was initially a simple 1,000-foot-long structure consisting of a slender 13-foot-wide neck terminating in a 40-foot-wide pier head before the shore end was widened between 1910 and 1912 to house a theatre and cinema complex with twelve shops. In 1951, a 10¼-inch miniature railway was laid along the pier deck by Charlie Kunz, who used a replica LNER 4-6-2 A4 Pacific locomotive named *Southern Belle* (see above) to pull the carriages, which could seat up to forty people. By the early 1960s, No. 619 *Santa Fe* was being used (see below), yet the line had ceased to run by the time the old pier pavilion on the pier head (opened in 1900) was severed from the remainder of the pier during a storm in November 1964 and fell into the sea four months later.

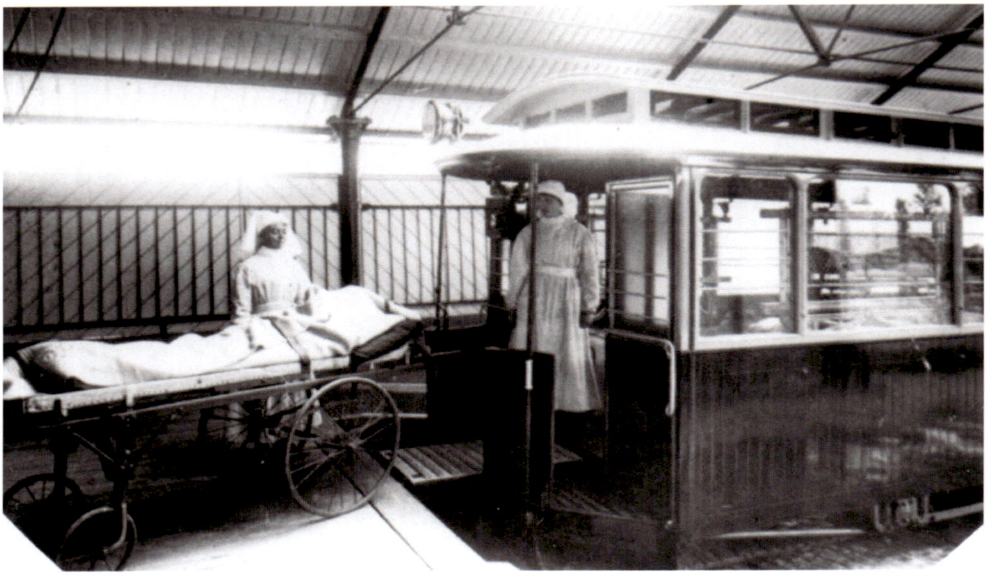

Above: **Dartford**

Four smallpox hospitals situated by the River Thames at Dartford were connected by a horse-drawn tram system, which ran on to the first section of a 300-foot pier with a floating pontoon. After being taken off the tramway car, the patients were wheeled down the pier's covered walkway to the pontoon and onto the ambulance steamers. The pier was in use until 1930, when the River Ambulance Service ceased, and was demolished in 1936.

Below: **Deal**

A tramway was used in the construction of Deal Pier and this was left in situ after the pier was opened on 14 July 1864 for the conveyance of goods, baggage and passengers. In 1872, a carriage called the 'Oversea Pilot' was provided on the tramway, which was propelled by means of a double-action treadle. Up to fourteen people could ride on it at a penny a head, but in the 1890s the tramway was discontinued and the track was removed.

Above: **Douglas Victoria**
Douglas Victoria Pier was opened on 1 July 1872 and in May 1902 the Douglas Horse Tramway, opened on 7 August 1876, was extended to run onto the pier to allow steamer passengers to easily reach their hotels and boarding houses along the promenade. The pier extension ran for double track 110 feet beyond the pier buildings and a further 30 feet as a single line. In 1965, the pier frontage gained the striking Sea Terminal building and this is now the terminus for the horse tramway as use of the pier extension was largely discontinued in the 1970s, although the track was retained for special occasions.

Below: **Southsea Clarence**
Between 1865 and 1876, the horse trams of the Landport & Southsea Tramway terminated on the pier after journeying from Portsmouth Town station. The line had an unusual track gauge of 4 feet 7 inches to enable standard-gauge wagons to be hauled.

Felixstowe (New)

The Coast Development Company built Felixstowe's second pier in 1905 to enable its famous Belle Steamers on the London–Great Yarmouth route to call at the resort area of the town rather than the old Great Eastern Railway pier in the dock area. The pier was constructed by Rogers Brothers to a length of 2,793 feet and it had a 3-foot 6-inch-gauge electric tramway along its north side with open-sided toast-rack vehicles. For the cost of 1*d.*, the tramway saved a walk of over half a mile to the pier head. The toast-rack carriages were decked out in a smart brown and cream livery and could each seat thirty-six people. The postcard above shows the tram cars, bedecked with flags, on the pier's opening day on 1 July 1905 when both the *Woolwich Belle* and *Walton Belle* called at the pier. The postcard below was sent in 1914 and shows three of the tram cars at the shore end of the wooden pier.

Felixstowe (New)
One of the toast-rack carriages of the Felixstowe Pier electric tramway pictured with its driver at the shore end platform in the 1930s.

Felixstowe (New)

The photograph above is an unusual postcard view of Felixstowe New Pier in 1914 showing one of the toast-rack cars at the shore-end station. In 1922, the pier was acquired by East Coast Piers Limited upon the winding up of the Coast Development Company, and four years later they purchased the ex-Ipswich tramcar No. 34 (built by Brush in 1904) and used the lower deck as a waiting area on the pier head. This can be seen in the photograph below. One of the original pier tram bodies was then fitted to the chassis, but the other car was scrapped in 1931. Upon the commencement of the Second World War, the tramway was closed on 10 September 1939, and in the following year the pier was breached as a defence measure. By the war's end it was in a poor state, and as only the shore end of the structure was restored, there was no longer a need for the pier tramway.

Above: **Great Yarmouth Wellington**

In 1948–49, the gardens of Great Yarmouth's Wellington Pier were home to a short-lived miniature railway operated by showman William Botterill and his Botterill's Miniature Railways Limited. The Wellington Pier line was operated in conjunction with the *News Chronicle* newspaper, which was advertised on the train carriages. Engine No. 1944 was employed on the railway, which operated between Whitsun and September.

Below: **Lowestoft South**

A 10¼-inch-gauge miniature railway was opened on Lowestoft's South Pier on Whitsun Bank Holiday Monday 17 May, 1948 and was operated by George Dingle from 1948 to 1951 using his locomotive 4-6-2 No. 1003 *Tamar Queen*. The council took over the line in 1952 and used locomotive 4-6-0 No. 45059 *Sonia* and four coaches purchased from the G&S Light Engineering Company. The pier railway closed in 1954.

Herne Bay

Herne Bay's first pier was opened to a length of 3,633 feet in 1832 and in the following year it acquired a sail-driven and manually propelled vehicle dubbed *Old Neptune's Car* (as pictured above). This ran on the pier until the wooden structure was declared unsafe in 1862 and closed. The pier was replaced by a small iron pier in 1873, which by 1899 had been substantially increased in length to 3,787 feet. A tramway used during the construction was utilised to run an electric tram to carry passengers to the steamers at a penny a time. The tram cars were powered through a third rail, which consisted of a groove in the deck with a conduit below and the power, supplied by a gas engine and generator situated in the pavilion, was taken up into the vehicle by a projecting arm situated underneath. The photograph below shows tram car No. 2 and its crew of two at the pier head in 1905.

Herne Bay

The tram stock was soon supplemented by two lighter vehicles, originally Bristol horse trams, adapted to travel fore and aft with the main vehicle. A small trolley was also coupled on for baggage. Unfortunately, on 16 July 1901, the trolley attached to the front of the tram jumped the rails and went over the side of the pier, dragging one of the light cars with passengers aboard with it (as shown in the photograph above). A seventy-four-year-old lady named Mrs Pearce was killed in the accident, and the inquest ruled that the pushing of a trolley in front of the cars should be discontinued. The tram car seen on the beach (No. 3) was soon put back on the pier and into service. The postcard below shows the petrol-electric tramcar, built locally by the Strode Engineering Works, introduced in August 1925 by the pier owners Herne Bay Urban District Council, who had acquired the pier in 1909.

Herne Bay

However, the Strode car proved to be unreliable and in 1934 it was relegated to running in tandem with a battery car, as pictured above at the pier head in 1938. The two gaps blown in the pier during the Second World War as a defence measure were only closed with wooden bridges, meaning that tramway could no longer operate, and in 1950 the rolling stock was sold for scrap. However, a miniature railway was run by locomotive builder J. N. Liversage from 1948 for three seasons on the section of the pier between the bridges. His line was laid between the tracks of the old tramway to a gauge of 7¼ inches and 2-6-0 tender locomotive *Teddy*, 0-6-0 *Topsy*, and a scale model of WD 2-10-0 *Longmoor* were used to pull the open truck and seated carriages. The postcard below shows Mr Liversage and *Topsy* pulling a train composed of small wagons and an open toast-rack type carriage.

Hunstanton

The tall and graceful pier at Hunstanton was opened on Easter Sunday, April 1870, to a length of 830 feet, and on 28 June 1947 a 9¼-inch miniature railway was opened on the pier by the Hunstanton Pier Company. The line ran for about 650 feet in the middle of the pier and had no proper stations at either end. A ride on it cost *6d.*, and the locomotive usually hauled the train to the pier head and propelled it back. The railway did not run during the 1950 season, and from 1951 it was operated by Botterill's Amusements, who used a Bassett Lowke 4-4-0 Midland Compound (seen in both of these postcards) and 4-6-0 Saint Class *Hampton Court* to pull three twelve-seater open bogie carriages. By 1954, the railway was being operated by John W. Harris Amusements and it was featured in the Ealing Studios comedy *Barnacle Bill* (or *All At Sea*), starring Alec Guinness, that was shot on the pier in 1956.

Hunstanton

In 1958, the Hunstanton Pier railway was acquired by Charles Reed to use on his 10¼-inch railway in Cassiobury Park, Watford. The track on Hunstanton Pier was also re-laid to 10¼-inch gauge at the same time, and the line continued to be operated by John W. Harris Amusements, who used a replica of a LNER 4-6-2 A4 Class Pacific called *Speed Ace* (it had formerly run on the Bognor Regis Pier miniature railway under the name *Southern Belle*), which is probably pulling the train in both of these photographs. The kiosks added for the *Barnacle Bill* film in 1957 can be seen in the lower view. At the end of the 1961 season, the line was closed and an increasing emphasis on providing entertainments at the pier's shore-end amusement centre led to the remainder of the structure being neglected. On 11 January 1978, the pier met its end when storm-force winds and high seas sent it crashing into the sea.

Hythe

In 1870, the Hythe and Southampton Pier and Steam Ferry Company was formed to provide a pier at Hythe for the ferry service to Southampton. The pier, designed by James Wright and John Dixon to a length of 2,100 feet and erected by Messrs Bergheim, was opened on New Year's Day 1881. The principal function of the pier was as a landing stage for the ferry, and the baggage of the ferry passengers was transported up and down the pier in hand carts (whose metal wheels damaged the decking) until a narrow-gauge tramway was erected on its north side by local undertaker Edward Kingham in July 1909. This ran off centre down the north side of the 16-foot-wide pier and had had a stock of two hand-propelled, open-sided, four-wheeled trucks. The postcard above shows one of the pre-tramway hand carts, whilst the lower view shows the 1909 tramway with a loaded luggage trolley.

Hythe

In 1922, the baggage tramway was replaced with a 2-foot-gauge railway laid on the south side of the pier, powered by a 250V DC third rail. To operate the line, two Brush locomotives (a third was used for spares), built in 1917, were acquired from the MOD Avonmouth mustard gasworks and converted from battery to third rail operation. Four carriages, built by Baguley Cars Ltd of Burton-upon-Trent, were supplied by the Drewry Car Company, and a tank truck was obtained to transport fuel oil to the ferry boats. Two luggage trucks were retained from the old tramway. The line was opened in July 1922 and a fare of 1*d.* was levied for passengers who used it. Two driving carriages, with controls at the seaward end, were supplied in 1923 by Drewry. The postcard above shows one of the Brush locomotives and three carriages during the 1930s. The lower postcard shows the train in the 1950s.

Hythe

The pier and its railway remain virtually unchanged since the 1920s and are a delightful throwback to a bygone age. The pier is recognised in the *Guinness World Records* book as having the oldest continually operated pier train, which meets every ferry arriving from Southampton. In normal operation the single train is made up of one of the Brush locomotives propelling three passenger coaches, with a four-wheel flat car for baggage. The locomotive is always at the landward end, and one of the driving carriages at the sea end. The line also has a four-wheel oil tanker, used to carry fuel to the Hythe ferries. The postcard above shows the Hythe Pier electric railway in the 1960s, whilst the photograph below, taken in August 2023, sees the train trundling along the pier to meet the ferry. Blue Funnel Ferries Ltd took over the operation of the pier and ferry in 2017 and usually provide a thirty-minute service.

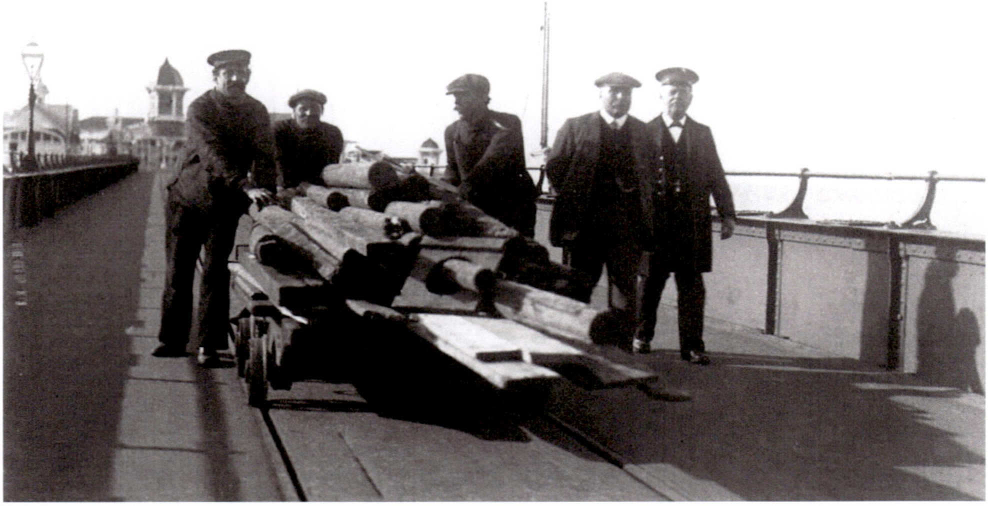

Margate

Designed by noted pier builder Eugenius Birch, Margate Jetty was opened on 9 April 1855 to a length of 1,240 feet and was the first major pier to be constructed of cast iron. It was extended in 1875–77 when the Jetty Extension was built to a design by George Gordon Page and a tramway laid along the pier to assist in the construction of the extension was retained to transport baggage and materials (as seen in the photograph above). The postcard below shows the 10¼-inch-gauge miniature railway that was opened on Margate's stone harbour pier in 1947 and ran on the upper level for 300 yards between the Droit Office and the lighthouse. The engine was modelled on an LMS *Royal Scot* locomotive and was named *Queen of Scots*, but by 1952 she had been replaced by a model of a Gresley Pacific. The rolling stock consisted of six twenty-seater open coaches.

Margate

In 1963, the harbour pier line was relocated to the adjoining iron pier (usually known as the 'Jetty'), although the steam engine was not moved to the jetty as it was deemed a fire risk, so a D1000 Western Independence diesel locomotive, built by David Curwen, was used instead. The railway continued in operation until the jetty was deemed unsafe and was closed in 1974. The railway was removed to the Payton Heights Railway in nearby Cliftonville.

Above: **Minehead**

Minehead Pier was opened on 25 May 1901 to a length of 750 feet and a tramway used in its construction was retained to carry baggage. It cost 2*d.* to transport up to 28 lb of baggage and 9*d.* to carry up to 2 cwt. However, the pier was never profitable and in May 1940 it was removed to allow gun batteries and searchlights a clear line of sight.

Below: **Rhyl**

Rhyl Pier was opened on 16 August 1867 to a length of 2,250 feet and a tramway was added to the pier in 1875 to transport baggage to the steamers, although the photograph below shows that an attractive passenger car was provided. The car was controlled and hand-propelled by staff using levers at the side of the vehicle and had seating for about four passengers and space for baggage. The tramway ran from the seaward side of the Bijou Pavilion and Baths to the end of the pier, but had been removed by the 1890s.

Ramsey

Ramsey Queens Pier on the Isle of Man was opened on 22 July 1886 to a length of 2,160 feet and a 3-foot-gauge tramway used in the construction of the pier was retained for use as a baggage line using seven four-wheeled trucks and one wagon propelled by hand. Following the completion of an extension to the pier (bringing its length to 2,248 feet) and a new landing stage in 1901, a hand-propelled car was purchased to transport passengers and their baggage along the pier. In 1937, the hand-propelled car was replaced by a Planet 4w 8-hp No. 2027 petrol locomotive, which pulled a toast-rack carriage, seating ten. This was joined in 1950 by a 10-hp Wickham railcar, powered by a Ford V8 petrol engine. This was provided by the Isle of Man Harbour Board, who added a turning loop for it. The postcard above shows the tramway track in 1902, and the lower view sees the Wickham railcar at the end of the pier.

Ramsey

On 10 September 1970, steamer calls at the pier ceased due to the poor condition of the wooden berthing head. The landing stage was fenced off in 1979 and two years later, on 9 September 1981, the tramway was closed by its operators, the Manx Electric Railway Society. That same year had seen the *Planet* locomotive rebuilt with a steam engine outline and this is currently on display in Jurby Transport Museum. The pier itself was closed in June 1991, although until 2003 it was allowed to be used for special open days. The first three restored sections of the Queens Pier were reopened in 2021 as part of a long-term restoration. The photograph above shows the Wickham railcar, complete with a fares board, by the pier head café in the 1960s, whilst the lower view shows both the railcar and the *Planet* locomotive at the pier entrance *c.* 1980.

Ramsgate

Mr W. M. C. Peatfield, of Broadstairs, originally suggested running a miniature railway along the East Pier of Ramsgate Harbour in the late 1930s, although by 1939 he was proposing to run it on the Western Undercliff. His railway failed to materialise, but a 10¼-inch line was operational for a short time on the East Pier in the 1950s–60s (pictured above). This ran along the length of the pier for a distance of about 1,300 feet and what looked like a steam locomotive pulled three articulated carriages. After the railway was removed, a land train ran along the pier for a time during the 1960s and this can be seen below. In 1969, a 5-inch-gauge steam- and electric-powered miniature railway was laid in Ellington Park by the Ramsgate and District Model Engineering Club, and this still runs on Sundays during the summer months (weather permitting).

Above: **Sheerness**

The original Sheerness Pier of 1835 suffered severe damage during a great storm on 29 November 1897 and was replaced by a new iron pier by Sheerness Council in 1899. The tramway used in the construction of the pier was retained as a baggage line for those using the steamers. This had a passing loop and terminated at a shelter on the pier head that doubled as a tea room. It appears to have fallen out of use early on.

Below: **Shotley Bristol**

The pier was erected in the 1894 by Lord Bristol opposite The Bristol Arms pub, which was named after him. The pier was constructed of wood to a length of about 500 feet and was used for row-boat ferries across the Orwell Estuary to Harwich. A tramway was provided to convey baggage, mail, and goods along the pier but, as was the case at Sheerness, it appears to have become disused.

Southend-on-Sea

Southend Pier was opened in June 1830 to a length of 600 feet, but it was too short, except at the highest of tides, to receive the steamers. In 1846, the pier was extended to 1¼ miles in length, making it the longest pier in Britain, and it was felt necessary to introduce a 3-foot-gauge tramway for hand-hauled, or, if windy, sail-driven luggage trucks. These can be seen in the photograph above from *c.* 1870. Horses were introduced onto the tramway in 1873 and two years later (upon the pier's acquisition by the Local Board) the wooden rails were re-laid in iron. Southend Local Board had purchased the pier on 1 July 1875 for £12,000 and upgraded the tramway, yet between 1881 and 1884, the line was closed due to the unsafe condition of the track, and by this time the pier itself was showing its age badly. The postcard below shows the horse tramway *c.* 1885.

Southend-on-Sea

A new iron pier was built between 1888 and 1890 to replace the old wooden one and a 3-foot 6-inch-gauge electric railway and generating plant was supplied by Messrs Crompton of Chelmsford. The first ¾-mile section was opened on 2 August 1890 using a toast-rack car with two trailers supplied by the Falcon works of Loughborough (the remaining ½ mile was opened the following year). The photograph above shows the car on the opening day. It was powered by a 13-hp motor taking 200V DC from the pier's generator and the current was collected from a centre rail and was returned through the running rails. A further car was acquired in 1893, and on 28 July 1898 the track acquired a passing loop at a cost of £4,100. Additional cars were ordered in 1902, 1909, and 1914, allowing seven-car trains to operate, each seating 250 passengers. The postcard below shows the toast-racks *c.* 1910.

Southend-on-Sea

The pier was extended further in 1898, bringing its length to 7,080 feet (1⅓ miles), and in 1902 it began receiving its electricity direct from Southend Corporation (at 500V DC), leading to the pier's generating plant being disposed of and the cars being upgraded with 18-hp motors. The track was doubled in 1931–32 and over 3.3 million people used the railway in 1947, but the old toast-rack trains were beginning to show their age. The corporation decided to introduce twenty-eight new enclosed electric trains (forming four seven-car units) for the 1949 season, manufactured by A. C. Cars Ltd of Thames Ditton at a cost of £99,100 (pictured above and below). They gave their customers a more comfortable ride, but had a fortunate escape when the Pier Pavilion was destroyed by fire on 6 October 1959 and only the prompt action of Pier Master Goble in driving away the trains saved them from also being incinerated.

Southend-on-Sea

The photograph above shows the sea-end railway station before the disastrous fire of 29 July 1976 destroyed the pier head. Two years later the pier railway was closed and in 1982 the cars were taken for scrap, although two of them were later purchased for the Southend Pier Museum. In 1984, it was announced that the pier railway would be restored with two new diesel-operated trains on a 3-foot-gauge single track with a passing loop. The new trains were built by Messrs Severn-Lamb Ltd of Stratford-upon-Avon and each comprised five aluminium bodies on steel frames. They were officially named *Sir William Heygate* and *Sir John Betjeman* after two staunch supporters of the pier. The railway was officially opened on 2 May 1986 by Princess Anne, who took the twelve-minute journey to the pier head. The new railway cost £223,627 and a new diesel train can be seen below.

Southend-on-Sea

On 9 October 2005, the pier head railway station was destroyed in another fire that ravaged the pier head. Nevertheless, the trains were soon running down the pier again to a temporary station, and they received a new blue and cream livery (matching that of Southend's buses). Work to repair the damaged pier head was commenced by contractors Nuttall John Marky in September 2008, which included rebuilding the station (as seen above), and the work was completed in 2010 at a cost of £2.4 million. In 2022, two new eco-friendly battery powered-trains, manufactured by Severn-Lamb as part of a £3-million investment package and clad in the old green and cream livery, were introduced to replace the 1986 units. They were named *Sir David Amess* (who was MP for Southend West from 1997 until his murder in 2021) and *William Bradley* (a former pier head keeper) and one is pictured below.

Southport

Southport Pier was opened on 2 August 1860 to a length of 3,600 feet and a line using manually propelled trucks to transport passengers and baggage was provided in 1863. This was replaced by a 3-foot 6-inch-gauge cable-operated tramway opened in 1865 (pictured above). A steam-operated 4-hp winding engine was provided halfway along the pier and the 3-foot 6½-inch-wire haulage cable was attached to two knife-board open cars that could each accommodate up to fifty passengers. The cable tramway was eventually replaced by an electric railway using the outside third rail system at 500V DC. Southport Corporation had been engaged to convert the tramway, and they also renewed the rolling stock with a new motor saloon powered by two 25-hp Westinghouse motors and two roofless trailers using existing bogie trucks of cars. The new line came into operation on 3 April 1905 and is pictured below.

Southport

The postcard above shows the electric railway on Southport Pier in 1918 with two open-top cars and one enclosed car. During the night of 3 July 1933, the pier head was destroyed by fire and the Southport Pier Company could not afford the repairs. In June 1936, the pier was sold to Southport Corporation for £34,744 and they immediately rebuilt the pier railway's rolling stock and a green-and-cream livery, inspired by the smart Blackpool Corporation tramway, was adopted. In 1950, on cessation of direct current electricity in the town, the Pier Committee of Southport Corporation decided to replace the DC electrically operated railway with a smaller one of 2-foot gauge. The new line opened for public use on 27 May 1950 and the photograph below shows a Hunslet 4245/50 4-4-0 on the pier on 4 November 1951.

Southport

Following an upgrade of the railway's rolling stock, the *Silver Belle*'s eight-car train commenced operations during the summer of 1954. This train consisted of a diesel-powered car at each end with four open and two closed cars marshalled intermediately, and is pictured above in around 1960. By the 1970s, the pier was facing difficulties due to falling customer revenue and following sixteen years of heavy usage, the continued operation of the pier railway was put in doubt in 1970. In the next two years, the *Silver Belle* was run with a smaller train until it was replaced in 1973 by a Bo-Bo diesel hydraulic locomotive named *English Rose*, which can be seen below in 1980. For much of the 1970s and 1980s the pier remained very much 'as it was', but fortunately a resolution to demolish it in 1990 was defeated by one vote. However, the railway ceased to run and the pier itself was closed in 1997 for safety reasons.

Southport

In 1998, the National Lottery granted £1.7 million towards the restoration of the pier and work commenced in 2000. The rebuilt pier was to be 3,462 feet long, built of steel, and feature a widened decking of hardwood, a new pavilion housing a café, and observatory centre, and a new pier tram. On May Day 2002, the pier was reopened to the public, and until the tram was ready a land train ferried people up and down the pier. The new pier tram finally came into operation on 22 August 2005. Seating eighty people, the tram was provided by UK Loco at a cost of £325,000. The final cost of restoring the pier was £7.2 million. However, in 2015, the tram was withdrawn due to council budget cuts and the cost of structural repairs to the pier caused by the tram. It was replaced by the pre-existing promenade land train. In 2022, the pier was closed again due to unstable decking.

Walton-on-the-Naze

Walton's second pier (following the building of the Old Pier in 1830) was opened in 1871 to a length of 530 feet. Between 1897 and 1899 the pier was greatly extended to a length of 2,610 feet by the Coast Development Company to enable their Belle Steamers, running between London and Great Yarmouth, to call at all states of the tide. The work was carried out by A. Fasey & Son of London and featured a south-facing curving pier head with three berths where both the London and Yarmouth boats terminated their services. To save steamer passengers a long walk, a single-track electric railway of 3-foot 6-inch gauge, running along the north side of the pier, was opened in June 1899. The rolling stock consisted of a motor car and two open-sided trailers, each with bench seating for thirty-two passengers. These two postcards by A. & G. Taylor show the pier railway's toast-rack-type carriages in 1907.

Walton-on-the-Naze

The staff operating the electric railway on Walton-on-the-Naze Pier pose for the postcard publisher *c.* 1910. The train consists of two toast-rack carriages, and the curved platform of the shore station can clearly be seen.

Walton-on-the-Naze

The open-sided cars of the electric railway on Walton-on-the-Naze Pier are seen at the pier head station in front of the pavilion on the above postcard from 1907. In 1935, the railway was dismantled upon the introduction of a battery car, which ran in a 6-foot-wide trough formed by narrow timber baulking fixed vertically to the decking. The toast-rack passenger car had seating for twenty people but the battery car was destroyed by fire on 30 May 1942. It was replaced by a Ford diesel locomotive (pictured below) that came from Wilson's pleasure railway at Allhallows in Kent. Known as *Dreadnought*, the loco pulled three toast-rack carriages, each seating eighteen, and ran on a 2-foot gauge from Easter to October each year until 1978 when it was taken out of service (and ended up on the Amerton Railway). It was replaced by a road train, which made occasional trips down the pier when required.

Weston-super-Mare Birnbeck

Weston-super-Mare Birnbeck is an unusual pier in that it connects to a small island, from which jetties were built to enable steamers to call. The pier was opened on 5 June 1867, and to assist those using the steamers, a baggage tramway, using a hand-propelled vehicle, was laid along the centre of the pier in 1884. This was extended around the north of the pavilion to help with the construction of the new low-water jetty, which was completed in 1898, and it was left in situ to carry baggage along the jetty. The top photograph shows two of the pier staff with the hand-propelled vehicle of the baggage tramway, whilst the baggage's owner has also decided to make use of the tramway! The lower image shows the pier staff unloading stone from the tramway by the lifeboat station situated on Birnbeck Island. Both photographs date from *c.* 1890.

Weston-super-Mare Birnbeck

For a short period during the 1930s, a passenger vehicle with knife-board seating, rather resembling a milk float, ran along the pier tramway. This was probably hand-propelled too and can be seen in the view above at the pier entrance. The line survived the Second World War when the pier was requisitioned by the military and used as a secret base for scientists to develop weapons of war, but was removed when the dilapidated pier was refurbished with £34,000 of compensation money. For one season in 1977, the pier was home to a miniature railway (seen left) using stock purchased at an auction of the Axe & Lym Valley's Light Railway. A Minirail Bo-Bo diesel called *The Cub* trundled along the 300 yards of track pulling two coaches. The pier closed in 1994, but there are plans by the local council to restore this historic and unusual seaside pier.

Weston-super-Mare Grand

Weston-super-Mare's second pier, the Grand, was officially opened on 11 June 1904 to a length of 1,080 feet, although it was intended to extend it as soon as possible to enable steamers to call. An area on the southern side of the pier was laid aside for an electric tramway and in 1905 work began on extending the pier by a further 1,213 feet, bringing its total length to 2,293 feet. The southern side of the extension was also left open for the proposed tramway, but permission to build it was never granted, and the extension itself was removed in 1920 as very few steamers ever called as it was too difficult to do so. The space allocated for the never-built tramway can be seen on the above postcard sent in 1908. The Grand Pier did, however, acquire the *Silver Arrow* land train in the 1950s, shown on the postcard below, and a land train continues to run along the pier today.

Brighton & Rottingdean Seashore Electric Railway

The Brighton & Rottingdean Seashore Electric Railway, affectionately known as the 'Daddy-long-legs', was an extraordinary railway that ran through the sea between piers at Brighton and Rottingdean. The splendid passenger vehicle, christened *Pioneer*, was a combination of a tram, boat and seaside pier, and it was powered like a tramway using electricity (originally provided by a generator under Rottingdean Pier) supplied to an overhead cable supported by wooden poles placed along the length of the line. The cable would be in contact with the wheels of the twin trolley poles of the passenger car for continual positive and return current through the vehicle, which ran upon two parallel lines of rails laid 18 feet apart, forming a single railway of 2-foot 8½-inch gauge. This unique railway ran for just four years from 1896 to 1900, and was officially closed in 1902.

Pier Railways Connected to the National Network

Oban

The railway pier at Oban photographed during the 1920s. The pier was opened on 1 July 1880 by the Callender & Oban Railway to connect with the ferry services to the Inner and Outer Hebrides and was built on reclaimed land. In 1903, the pier was enlarged and two extra platforms were provided with the opening of the line from Connel Ferry to Ballachulish. Despite being a listed building, the original station building was demolished to make way for a rationalised station, opened on 3 January 1986. Known as the 'Gateway to the Isles', the pier is owned by Caledonian Maritime Assets Limited, and the railway station, is the terminus of the West Highland line from Glasgow Queen Street station. The ferry terminal adjoins the station and Caledonian MacBrayne ferries sail to Tiree, Lismore, Islay, Coll, Colonsay, Craignure (Mull), Castlebay (Barra), and Lochboisdale (South Uist).

Above: **Aberdyfi/Aberdovey**
This small Welsh pier, opened in 1882 to a length of 370 feet, supported a double-track railway connected to the main line, turntable, and three landing stages on different levels where timber, slate, railway sleepers, coal, potatoes, and livestock were landed. The rails were removed before a new pier of 240 feet in length was opened in 1972.

Below: **Ardrossan Montgomerie**
Ardrossan Harbour was served by two railways: the Caledonian to Montgomerie Pier (opened in 1888 and pictured *c* .1902) and the Glasgow and South Western to Winton Pier (opened in 1892). Both piers offered boat services to Arran. Winton Pier was to become the favoured rail and boat head and regular railway passenger services to Montgomerie Pier ceased in 1932. All boat services were centred on Winton Pier from 1968, and a new station called Ardrossan Harbour was opened on 19 January 1987.

Above: **Balloch**
Balloch Pier was opened in 1850 on the shore of Loch Lomond in Scotland to serve the steamer services following the extension of the Dumbarton & Balloch Joint Railway from Balloch Town. This postcard shows the pier in 1904 and the landing pontoon for the steamers was located on its western side. The station was closed on 29 September 1986, although the pier remains, and the steamer *Maid of the Loch* is berthed there.

Below: **Banavie**
The pier station at Banavie was opened on 1 June 1895 to serve the paddle steamers that operated on the Caledonian Canal in Scotland and was reached by a short branch from the Fort William to Mallaig line. The pier itself was a short and wide plain wooden structure sited immediately opposite the station. Banavie Pier station was closed to passengers in 1939 and goods in 1951, and the pier was subsequently removed.

Above: **Bantry**
Bantry Pier was the terminus of the Cork Bandon & South Coast Railway's main line from Cork from June 1909, when the CB&SCR extended the railway from Bantry Town and constructed a platform and station building. Steps led down from the station to the ferry landing stage. Passenger trains to the pier were terminated by the Great Southern Railway in September 1938 and goods services ceased in 1949. Bantry Town was closed on 1 April 1961.

Below: **Schull**
The west of Ireland was home to a number of small harbour piers with rail connections for goods traffic, including Schull, County Cork (pictured below), served by the Schull & Skibbereen Tramway & Light Railway Company for fish traffic between 1893 and 1947. Similar rail-connected harbour piers for goods traffic in Ireland included those at Baltimore, Cappagh, Courtmacsherry, Fahan, Fenit, Killybegs, and Rathmullen.

Above: **Barry**

A branch line off the Barry Railway, opened in 1896, ran through a 280-yard tunnel to terminate at a station on Barry Island with a landing stage and passenger pier, officially opened on 21 July 1899. The pier was available at all states of the tide for the Bristol Channel steamer traffic and was reached from the railway station by a covered gangway and hydraulic lift. The pier pontoon was removed in 1975, and the branch line was closed on 5 July 1976.

Below: **Burnham-on-Sea**

The jetty/slipway at Burnham-on-Sea was built for the broad-gauge Somerset Central Railway and it was opened along with the railway on 3 May 1858. A siding from Burnham station ran onto the jetty, which was used by paddle steamers to take railway passengers to Cardiff. However, the jetty proved very difficult for the steamers to use, and the last one called in 1909. The siding to the jetty was removed in the 1920s.

Above: **Broughty Ferry**
Broughty Ferry Pier station was opened by the Dundee & Arbroath Railway on 17 May 1848 and in 1850 the pier housed Thomas Bouch's second 'floating railway' (the first train ferry in the world), which ran across the Tay between Broughty Ferry and Tayport. The service ceased on 1 June 1878 upon the opening of Bouch's Tay Railway Bridge, but following the bridge's collapse during a storm on 28 December 1879 with the loss of seventy-five lives, it was used again between 1880 and 1887. The view above is *c.* 1890s.

Below: **Craigendoran**
Craigendoran Pier was opened by the Caledonian Railway on 15 May 1882 for the North British Steam Packet Company's services to Rothesay. The pier station, which was situated alongside the main Craigendoran station, had a long, single, curving platform on the north side of a run-round loop. The station was closed in 1972.

Dover Admiralty

The Admiralty Pier at Dover was opened to a length of 800 feet in 1854 and the South Eastern Railway (which had reached Dover in 1844) extended their line onto a station on the pier in 1861. The rival London, Chatham & Dover Railway opened its line to Dover on 22 July 1861, and on 1 November 1861 this was extended to a new station called Dover Harbour close to Town station. However, the LC&DR passengers had to walk along the Admiralty Pier to reach the ferries until 30 August 1864 when both railway companies were allowed to extend their services along the newly enlarged pier, although they had separate platforms and there was only just room for a double-track line. The Admiralty extended the pier for a further 1,000 feet to a length of 2,100 feet at a cost of £693,077, which was completed on 30 March 1875. These two postcards of the pier date from *c.* 1900 to 1910.

Dover Admiralty

Between 1893 and 1919 the Admiralty Pier was lengthened to 4,140 feet as part of the Admiralty Harbour scheme and widened at the shore end to accommodate the new Dover Marine station, which replaced the cramped old station on the pier. Sir Percy Crosland Tempest designed the new station with a stone frontage, four railway tracks, and two island platforms covered by a 770-foot-long braced arch roof. Access to the landing stages from the station was via covered walkways. The new station was opened for passenger traffic on 18 January 1919. The Southern Railway commenced a train ferry service from the pier on 12 October 1936, but this ceased in 1994. Dover Marine station was renamed Dover Western Docks on 14 May 1979, but this too was closed on 24 September 1994. Both the Admiralty Pier and the former Marine station have Grade II listed status.

Dover Prince of Wales

The Prince of Wales Pier was built to give shelter to the eastern side of the new Admiralty Harbour and was opened on 31 May 1902. Three landing stages were placed on the west side of the pier for cross-channel steamers, and these were joined by another placed on the eastern side in 1904 to be used as a berth for transatlantic liners. The same year saw an extension of the South Eastern & Chatham Railway from Dover Harbour station to the Prince of Wales Pier, and the first trial run to the pier took place on 25 June 1904. In 1918, a single-track railway was laid from the pier along the seafront to the Eastern Dockyard, and this was screened off from the promenade by a small fence. The line was to remain in use until December 1964, by which time buses had replaced trains on the pier. In 2016, the pier was closed and demolished for the redevelopment of the Western Docks.

Above: **Dun Laoghaire Carlisle**

The Carlisle Pier was opened in 1855 and four years later a branch off the Dublin to Wicklow Railway was extended on to it. The pier was used for both passenger and mail boat traffic, principally to Holyhead. On 11 October 1980, the pier station was closed as it could no longer accommodate the new DART electric trains, and the ferries also no longer run from the pier and use a new terminal nearer Dun Laoghaire station.

Below: **Rosslare**

The first Rosslare Pier station was opened by the Waterford & Wexford Railway in 1882 and served the steamer traffic to Fishguard Harbour. It was extended for the Great Western Railway and Great Southern & Western Railway in 1906 following the opening of the line to Abbey Junction (Waterford). The station was renamed Rosslare Harbour (Pier) in 1977 but it was closed on 14 September 1989 when a new shore station was opened.

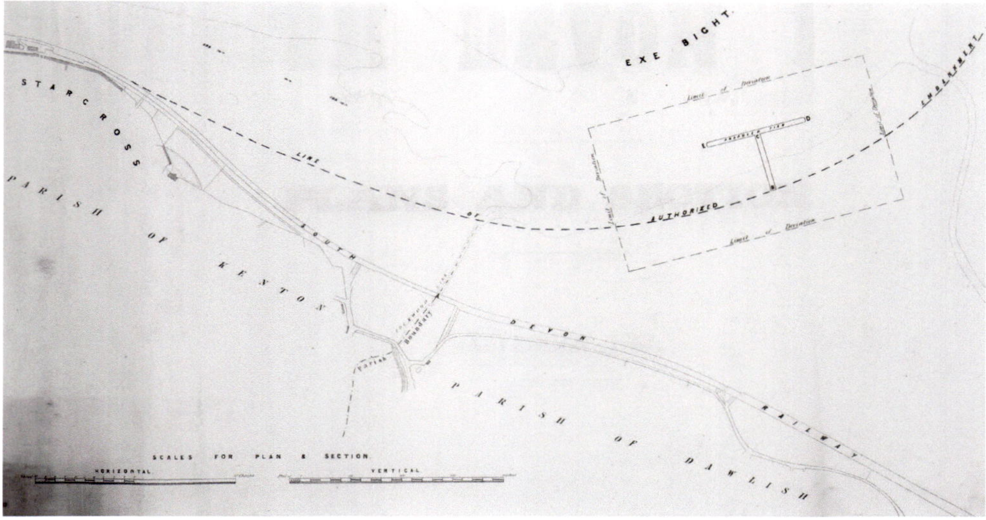

Above: **Exe Bight**

This very obscure pier served an oyster fishery on the River Exe in Devon and was served by a rail siding off the South Devon Railway between Starcross and Dawlish Warren. The pier was opened on 28 December 1868, but within a few weeks all the oysters had been killed during severe gales. The pier was thereafter occasionally used to land merchandise, but it was closed around 1875 and demolished in 1880.

Below: **Hampton-on-Sea**

The pier at Hampton-on-Sea, Herne Bay, was also used for an unsuccessful oyster fishery and had a horse tramway that was connected to the London, Chatham & Dover Railway. The pier was opened in July 1866, but the fishery soon foundered, and to make matters worse the pier caused the land to scour away on its western side and houses had to be demolished. The shore end of the pier can still be seen.

Above: **Fairlie**
Fairlie was connected to the Glasgow & South Western Railway on 1 July 1882 via a short branch line from the Ardrossan to Largs line. The branch terminated at a wooden pier with a covered island platform and walkway to the landing stage. Shipping services were provided to Millport, Bute, Campbeltown, and Arran until the 1960s but the pier station was officially closed on 31 July 1972. The pier was subsequently demolished.

Below: **Greenock Princes**
The Greenock & Ayrshire Railway was opened to Greenock Princes Pier in December 1869 and on 25 May 1894, the Glasgow & South Western Railway built a distinctive new station with six Italianate red-brick towers and verandah roofs. However, calls at the Princes Pier were reduced in favour of the more convenient rail head at Gourock Pier and in 1965 the railway was closed. The pier was demolished in 1969.

Felixstowe (Old)
The Old Pier at Felixstowe was the terminus of a branch line from Westerfield opened by the Felixstowe Railway & Pier Company on 1 May 1877, and a tramway was laid along the pier to assist in the construction of the railway before it was connected to the completed line. The railway and pier were promoted by 'Colonel' George Tomline (1813–89), MP for East Suffolk, but in 1879 the Great Eastern Railway began operating them and in 1887 they were purchased outright. From 1895 to 1930, the pier was used by the GER (and LNER from 1923) as a calling point for steamers from Ipswich and Harwich. However, traffic to the pier declined following the opening of Felixstowe Town station in 1898 and many services did not venture beyond the preceding Felixstowe Beach station. The pier station became unmanned and closure to passengers came on 30 June 1951.

Folkestone Harbour
The harbour at Folkestone was acquired in 1842 for £18,000 by the South Eastern Railway, who were in the process of building the London to Dover line through Folkestone, and on 1 August 1843, the SER opened a ferry service from Folkestone to Boulogne. A branch was laid down to the harbour from the main line and in 1849 it was extended across the inner harbour on a swing bridge to terminate at a station adjoining the ferry terminal. In 1861, a new 600-foot-long wooden pier was built to accommodate the ever-larger steamers and in 1876 the railway was extended onto the pier (above). In 1883, the pier was rebuilt in masonry to accommodate two railway lines, and further improvements were carried out between 1897 and 1905 when the pier was extended to its current length of 1,480 feet (pictured below) and Folkestone Harbour station (see opposite page, above) was rebuilt.

Folkestone Harbour

Although always second in importance to Dover, Folkestone Harbour continued to be a popular alternative cross-channel ferry port, but in 1984, following privatisation of BR subsidiary Sealink, it passed out of railway hands to Sea Containers of Bermuda for £66 million. In 1990, the Swedish shipping giant Stena acquired the ferry service but they closed the Folkestone–Boulogne route on 31 December 1991. Sea Containers reopened the crossing on 11 April 1992 with a Hoverspeed Sea Cat service but this ceased on 1 October 2000. On 2 July 2004, Sea Containers sold the Port of Folkestone to Roger De Haan's Folkestone Harbour Company for £11 million. The harbour branch line continued to receive the Orient Express (see below) and steam charter trains until 2009 and it was officially closed on 31 May 2014. Both the pier and the station have since been restored for leisure use.

Above: **Fort Augustus**
Fort Augustus Pier was located at the southern end of Scotland's famous Loch Ness and was used for ferry services to Inverness. The railway station was opened by the Highland Railway on 22 July 1903 as a summer-only extension from Fort Augustus station on the Invergarry & Fort Augustus Railway. The pier station had a station building and run-round loop but it proved to be poorly patronised and was closed on 30 September 1906.

Below: **Kentallen**
The station at Kentallen on the Ballachulish branch of the Callander & Oban Railway was opened on 24 August 1903 and a goods-only line ran down to the adjacent stone pier on the southern shore of Loch Linnhe. Steamers on the Oban to Fort William service called at the pier, but it never became a major interchange. The station closed for good on 28 March 1966, but the station building has been converted into a hotel and restaurant.

Fort William

Fort William's Town Pier on Loch Linnhe in Scotland, which dated back to the early nineteenth century, was served by the West Highland Railway from 7 August 1894, and by the steamers of Caledonian MacBrayne, which sailed to Oban and as far afield as Glasgow. The above view of the pier dates from 1953 and shows a fine array of coaches waiting to receive the passengers from the vessel *Loch Fyne* and the Caledonian MacBrayne ferry terminal. The pier station closed on 9 June 1975 (when the station was relocated to the eastern end of the town), and the view below shows it just before closure. The pier is still used for cruises during the summer months, and it houses a popular restaurant located in the former bait shed. Fort William has a second pier, built in 1927 with a 3-foot-gauge railway for the delivery of alumina and the dispatch of the finished aluminium. Closure of the aluminium works occurred in 1977, but the pier remains and houses an underwater centre.

Gourock

The harbour at Gourock was purchased by the Caledonian Railway in 1869 but it was to be another twenty years before they built a railway to it, which terminated on a new steamboat wharf and pier, opened on 1 June 1889. The Caledonian Steam Packet Company was formed to run steamers from the pier, which became their headquarters (and that of their successor Caledonian MacBrayne) and the principal rail head in the Firth of Clyde. In 1971, a link span was installed for the ferry service to Dunoon, but in the 1980s the western end of the railway station was cut back by eighteen bays and the glazed canopies over the platforms were taken down. The pier was also cut back. Eventually, a new station was officially opened on 1 August 2012. Caledonian MacBrayne no longer operates a roll-on/roll-off service from the pier, although the pedestrian ferries to Dunoon continue to sail from it.

Granton

Granton Pier lies in the centre of Granton Harbour on the Firth of Forth and was completed to a length of 1,700 feet in October 1844. In the following year a steamer service was commenced to Stirling and across the Forth to Burntisland. During her first official visit to Edinburgh on 1 September 1842, Queen Victoria landed at the pier and was received by the Duke of Buccleuch, who wanted a rail connection to the harbour. He invested in the Edinburgh, Leith & Newhaven Railway, which opened a line on 31 August 1842 from Edinburgh Canal Street to Trinity, which was extended on to Granton Pier on 19 February 1846. Two years later the Edinburgh, Leith & Granton Railway (as it had been renamed) was absorbed by the Edinburgh & Northern Railway, who built a new station on the pier. Granton Pier station was closed to passengers from 2 November 1925, but goods services ran until 1986.

Granton (above) and Burntisland (below)

In a bid to improve the transfer of goods on and off the ferries between Granton and Burntisland, Thomas Bouch, the manager of the Edinburgh & Northern Railway (the Edinburgh, Perth & Dundee Railway from 1849), designed his 'floating railway', which consisted of moving inclined linkspan ramps fixed to a slipway, which were raised and lowered by a bascule powered by a stationery steam engine to accommodate the 20-foot difference between low and high tides. The rails on the ramps aligned with those on the piers and on the ferries to ensure a smooth transfer of wagons. On 3 February 1850, the first roll-on/roll-off train ferry in the world opened between Granton and Burntisland, where they connected with the EP&D's railway system. The opening of the Forth rail bridge on 4 March 1890 meant closure for the train ferry, although ferries ran between the two towns until 1953.

Above: **Holyhead Admiralty**

The Admiralty Pier at Holyhead was designed by civil engineer John Rennie to a length of 984 feet and was opened in 1821. Three timber jetty extensions were added in 1849 for the City of Dublin Steam Packet Company's services to Kingstown (Dun Laoghaire). In 1856, the pier station was connected to the Chester & Holyhead Railway, but on 1 April 1925 the LMS closed the station and demolished the timber extension structures.

Below: **Holyhead Breakwater**

The breakwater at Holyhead is the longest in the United Kingdom and was constructed to a length of 1.7 miles between 1848 and 1873. A 7-foot-gauge railway was used to convey stone from a quarry on Holyhead Mountain to build the breakwater and it was retained by the Board of Trade for maintenance use. In 1913, they converted it to standard gauge, and it was served by Wickham trollies and diesel locomotives.

Above: **Kyle of Lochalsh**

The railway from Dingwall to Strome Ferry was opened by the Dingwall & Skye Railway Company on 19 August 1870 but it was not extended to Kyle of Lochalsh to connect with ferry services to Skye and the Outer Hebrides until 2 November 1897. Slipways were later added to the pier for the roll-on/roll-off car ferry services to Kyleakin in Skye, but they ceased following the transfer of the Outer Hebrides services to Ullapool and the opening of the bridge to Skye on 16 October 1995. Both the pier and station are listed buildings.

Below: **Strome Ferry**

The pier at Strome Ferry (or Stromeferry) was used for steamer services to isles of Skye (Portree) and Lewis (Stornoway), but its importance declined after the railway was extended to Kyle of Lochalsh and the majority of the ferry services were transferred there. The pier was demolished in 1937, but the station remains open.

Above: **Larne**
Larne Harbour railway station was opened on a quay-like pier structure on 1 October 1862 as the terminus of the railway from Carrickfergus and Belfast. Steamer services ran to Stranraer, and in 1890 the station was resited and rebuilt with a covered station building with a double-faced platform: one serving the still-open Belfast line, and the other the closed 3-foot narrow-gauge line from Ballymena. Ferry services now run to Cairnryan.

Below: **Stranraer**
Stranraer Harbour railway station was opened by the Portpatrick Railway on 1 October 1862, and ten years later on 1 July 1872, the ferry service to Larne in the north of Ireland was commenced from the pier. The pier and station were subsequently enlarged, which saw the station have two main platforms and a bay platform on the west side. However, the ferry services were transferred to Cairnryan in 2011, although the station remains open.

Lymington

On 12 July 1858, the privately owned Lymington Railway reached the town via a branch from Brockenhurst on the London & South Western Railway's line from London to Bournemouth and in 1861 the railway company opened a small jetty down river from the Town Quay, easing somewhat the problems of access to the town at low tide. On 23 March 1878, the Lymington Railway was acquired by the L&SWR and on 1 May 1884 they constructed a ½-mile branch from the town station to a new pier, thus allowing sailings to Yarmouth to be undertaken at all states of the tide. The L&SWR also took over the steamer services by acquiring for £2,750 the vessels of the Solent Steamship Company. In 1923, the railway, pier, and ferries became part of the newly formed Southern Railway, who built new slipways that were adjacent to Lymington Pier for the car ferry *Lymington*, which began running on 1 May 1938.

Lymington

Upon Nationalisation of the railways in 1948, the diesel-electric paddle vessel *Farringford* was introduced to partner *Lymington*. By 1955 42,000 cars were being carried annually on the route and a third car ferry, *Freshwater*, entered service on 21 September 1959 with a capacity of 620 passengers and twenty-six cars. The three vessels remained in service until 1973 when the C Class ferries, named *Caedmon*, *Cenwulf*, and *Cenred*, were introduced. The railway to the pier was electrified on 2 June 1967 and a new £250,000 terminal was opened in January 1976, which was placed on reclaimed land just to the east of the pier along with a new linkspan to allow easier berthing and loading/unloading. To accommodate the linkspan the pier was shortened by about 60 feet. Wightlink now operate the crossing and in 2008 they replaced the C Class ferries with the Wight Class *Wight Light*, *Wight Sky*, and *Wight Sun*.

Above: **Milford Haven Newton Noyes**
The 900-foot-long Milford Haven Newton Noyes Pier and Railway were opened in 1872 for use of goods traffic, but the usage of the pier declined after the opening of the docks in 1888. The pier was thereafter used occasionally for steamship traffic, and by a shipbreakers and the Admiralty. It remains, although much altered.

Below: **Neyland**
Neyland (originally called New Milford) was chosen by the South Wales Railway as the port for the Irish Sea mail vessels and a commodious station was opened on 15 April 1856. Adjoining the station was a pontoon pier with rails laid for wagons. The GWR opened its marine factory at Neyland but this was closed in 1906–07 after the transfer of the Irish sailings to Fishguard. The railway to Neyland was closed on 14 June 1964, and the ferry services ceased in March 1975 following the opening of the Cleddau Bridge.

New Holland

New Holland Pier station was opened by the Manchester, Sheffield & Lincolnshire Railway on 1 March 1848 and was situated at the end of a 1,375-foot-long pier, from where ferries steamed across the Humber to Hull from a pontoon landing stage added in December 1849. Upon Grouping in 1923, the pier and railway passed into the hands of the London & North Eastern Railway, who carried out major improvements to the pier, including replacing its wooden substructure, adding an extra railway track, and the provision of a new floating pontoon in 1935 to accommodate the recently introduced car-carrying paddle steamers *Tattershall Castle* and *Wingfield Castle*. They were joined by the *Lincoln Castle* in 1940. The train service to the pier ceased on 24 June 1981 with the opening of the Humber Bridge but the pier escaped demolition and is used for the shipping of grain and other cargoes.

Piel

Situated 3 miles south of Barrow-in-Furness, Piel Pier was officially opened on 24 August 1846 along with the opening of the Furness Railway to the pier from Dalton through Rampside. The pier extended 1,500 feet from Roa Island into the Piel Channel – the first 810-foot section of the pier led to an extension on differing levels offering three landing stages available at all states of the tide for the Fleetwood steamers. However, this meant that the steamer passengers had a walk of 700 feet to the far end landing stage from the pier railway station. The railway ran onto the pier via the embankment which connected Roa to the mainland. In 1868, a new curved pier was built, but all steamer services ceased in 1881 with the opening of the Ramsden Dock station and ferry terminal at Barrow. Piel station was relocated to the shore and stayed open until 1936. Piel Pier was demolished in 1891.

Above: **Portsmouth Harbour**

The extension of the L&SWR and LB&SCR Joint Railway to Portsmouth Harbour was opened on 2 October 1876 and the station was constructed on wooden piles, later replaced by iron supports. Landing stages were provided for the Isle of Wight and Gosport ferries, and a slipway for the floating bridge (1840–1959). Portsmouth Harbour station remains busy as a railway connection to the Isle of Wight and Gosport ferries.

Below: **Southampton Royal**

This pier was opened in 1833 for boat services and in 1847 a horse tramway connected the pier to Southampton railway station. The tramway was replaced by railway onto the pier in 1876, which terminated in a single platformed station, although there were limitations on the weight of the train. The station was rebuilt with two platforms housing canopy shelters in 1892 but it was officially closed in 1921.

Port Victoria

The 561-foot-long wooden pier at Port Victoria was opened by the South Eastern Railway on 11 September 1882 as the terminus of its branch from Hoo Junction. Situated on the isolated Isle of Grain, the railway ran on to the end of the pier to connect with a ferry service to Sheerness. The pier's isolation also led it to be used by European royalty (including Queen Victoria) as a favoured landing place close to London. The line had been built by the SER to counter the rival service provided by its fierce rival, the London, Chatham & Dover Railway, from Queenborough Pier, which had opened in 1876. According to the SER, the opening of Queenborough Pier had violated the Continental Trade Agreement between the two companies to share all receipts from Kent coast and Continental traffic. The pier's wooden supports proved appetising to marine worms and they had to be encased in concrete in 1901.

Port Victoria

In addition to being eaten by marine worms, the pier was damaged on 27 May 1915 when the minesweeper *Princess Irene* blew up in the Medway Estuary with great loss of life. This led to the seaward end of the structure being declared unsafe and in 1916 it was closed, which meant all trains now had to terminate at the shore end of the pier. In 1932, the pier was totally closed, and the railway station was relocated on land. The station buildings on the pier were demolished in 1933, and in 1941 most of the structure was removed by the Admiralty, for which the Southern Railway received £841 in compensation. The lonely Port Victoria station finally closed on 10 June 1951, when the area was acquired for a large oil refinery and was replaced by a new station at Grain. However, passenger services on the branch were withdrawn from 2 December 1961, although the line remains open for freight.

Queenborough

Port Victoria's rival pier on the other side of the Medway Estuary at Queenborough on the Isle of Sheppey was opened on 15 May 1876 by the London, Chatham & Dover Railway for a passenger ferry and mail service to Flushing (now Vlissingen) in Holland provided by the Zeeland Steamship Company. The pier was located at the end of a ¾-mile branch off the Sittingbourne–Sheerness line, which had been opened on 19 June 1860. The Flushing–Queenborough service proved to be an immediate success, leading to the commencement of day and night services on 1 June 1887. However, the pier suffered two devastating fires in 1882 and 1900, and the ferries often had difficulty navigating the narrow Medway Estuary sandbanks, leading to the night service being transferred to Folkestone on 1 May 1911. The day service continued to use Queenborough Pier until November 1914.

Queenborough

The Flushing services never returned to Queenborough after the First World War. The abandoned Queenborough Pier now saw only occasional use as a cargo berth, although in 1926 the pier was used by 600 soldiers of the 78th Highlanders who arrived by special trains from Dover with their wives and children and were transferred to the troopship *Assistance*. However, by 1933 the pier lay virtually unused with its wooden piles being eaten away by toredo worms. During the Second World War it was used as a base for minesweepers, but became derelict in the years following the war and partially collapsed. The owners, British Railways, lifted the railway track in 1955 and then engaged contractors John Mowlem to commence demolition of the pier using floating cranes to remove the decaying wooden piles. The work was started in September 1955 and was completed the following year.

River Severn: New Passage (Above) and Portskewett (Below)
The Bristol & South Wales Union Railway built the 11½-mile broad-gauge railway from Bristol to New Passage Pier from where steamers took passengers across the River Severn to Portskewett Pier in Monmouthshire, where their journey would recommence by train. New Passage Pier was officially opened on 25 August 1863 with a length of nearly 1,800 feet and it had a 300-foot-long railway platform for passengers with offices and a waiting room. At Portskewett the 708-foot-long pier was opened on 1 January 1864 at the end of a short branch line from Portskewett station. The Great Western Railway acquired the B&SWUR on 1 August 1868 and converted it to standard gauge in 1872–73. However, the opening of the Severn Tunnel on 1 December 1886 spelt the end for the two piers and their railways, and their demolition commenced in the autumn of 1887.

Ryde

The pier at Ryde on the Isle of Wight was built in 1814 and was subsequently lengthened to be available to use at all states of the tide. To assist passengers using the ferries, a tramway pier was built adjoining the original pier and was opened on 29 August 1864. Using horse power, the tramway had two running lines and platforms at both ends of the pier (above). On 1 August 1871, the tramway was extended along the Esplanade and through a private building to the Isle of Wight Railway at St John's Road, which had been opened to Shanklin on 23 August 1864 (an extension to Ventnor was carried out two years later). The tramway extension was closed in 1880 upon the opening of the extension of the Isle of Wight Railway to Ryde Pier Head. The tramway was electrified (below) on 4 June 1886 and trundled up and down the pier providing a useful service until it ran for the last time on 27 January 1969.

Ryde

The extension of the Isle of Wight Railway to Ryde Esplanade and Ryde Pier Head was opened in 1880 by the London & South Western Railway and London, Brighton & South Coast Railway. The double-track railway adjoined the other two piers on its own pier, and culminated in three platforms at the pier head with two of them on an island platform. The station buildings were at right angles to the line of the railway. Seven landing stages were provided for the ferries operated by the LB&SCR and L&SWR Joint Committee. The photograph above shows Ryde Pier Head station soon after it was opened on 12 July 1880, whilst the postcard below shows Ryde Pier in 1909 with the promenade pier on the left, the tramway pier in the middle, and the railway pier on the right. Ryde Esplanade station (opened on 5 April 1880) is in the foreground and Ryde Pier Head station centre right.

Ryde

In 1923, all of the island's railways came under the grouping of the newly formed Southern Railway, who wanted total control of the pier to avoid the payment of tolls to the Ryde Pier Company. In 1924, the promenade and tramway piers were sold to the SR for £84,000 and the RPC was wound up. Steamer services from the pier also came under the control of the SR, who introduced new steamers named after locations on the Isle of Wight. The railways were nationalised on 1 January 1948 and British Railways took over both the steamer services and the pier. The photograph above, taken in 1965, shows both the railway and tramway, the latter with one of the Drewry Railcars introduced in 1927. Originally petrol driven, they were converted to diesel running in 1959. The photograph below was also taken in the 1960s and was taken from the tramway, closed in 1969, looking towards the shore.

Ryde

By 1966, only the line between Ryde Pier Head and Shanklin remained open and this was electrified with 660V DC third rail system for use by ex-London Transport Standard Stock Tube trains. They were introduced in March 1967 (see above) and were designated as British Rail Class 485 and 486. Ryde Pier Head station was reconstructed with two tracks and three platform faces, but only one track and platform face is now in use by the railway's current operator, Island Line (part of the franchise operated by South Western Railway). In 2021, Vivarail D-Train Class 484 EMUs, converted from London Underground D78 stock, were introduced to replace the 1989 Class 483 trains, and one of them can be seen below at Ryde Pier Head station in June 2022. Trains run every thirty minutes between Ryde Pier Head and Shanklin and at Smallbrook Junction they connect with the heritage Isle of Wight Railway.

Above: **Silloth**

A 1,000-foot-long timber piled pier was built in 1857 to protect the new deep-water dock developed by the Carlisle & Silloth Bay Railway Company at Silloth. The dock had an extensive railway system and a pair of tracks ran along the pier to carry freight, mainly propelled by horses. By 1900 the pier was principally being used for promenading, fishing, and as a base for boat trips; however, the last section of it was demolished in 1973.

Below: **Windermere Lakeside**

The pier and railway station at Windermere Lakeside in the Lake District were opened by the Furness Railway in June 1869 and a narrow-gauge tramway was used to transport coal from the station to the steamers. Trains were timed to coincide with sailings from the pier to Ambleside (Waterhead) and Bowness-on-Windemere. The pier and station are now part of the preserved Lakeside & Haverthwaite Railway.

Stokes Bay

The pier at Stokes Bay was the terminus of a branch built off the London & South Western Railway's Gosport line by the Stokes Bay Railway and Pier Company and was opened on 6 April 1863. The pier was 600 feet in length and had a commodious train shed for the passengers using the ferries to Ryde. In 1865, the pier and ferries passed to the Ryde Pier Company, before the railway and pier were acquired by the L&SWR in 1875. The pier station came under the responsibility of the stationmaster at Gosport and during the 1880s there were five steamer services daily in each direction, with three on Sundays, which were usually met by a train waiting on the pier. However, the opening of the railway to Portsmouth Harbour in 1876 diverted most of the traffic away and the Stokes Bay line was closed on 30 October 1915, with ferries having ceased two years later. The pier lasted until 1975.

Wemyss Bay

Wemyss Bay Pier and its railway station were opened on 15 May 1865 as the terminus of the Greenock & Wemyss Bay Railway. The pier had two steamer berths and the station two platforms. The Caledonian Steam Packet Company took over the running of the steamers from Wemyss Bay on 1 May 1890 and three years later, on 27 July 1893, the Greenock & Wemyss Bay Railway was amalgamated with the Caledonian Railway Company. The new owners widened the pier in 1902–03 and built a new station in half-timbered style with a covered curved roof of steel girders and glass and a 60-foot-high clock tower in Italianate style. During work to provide roll-on/roll-off facilities for the Rothesay car ferry, the pier suffered a fire on 1 March 1977 and the outer section was demolished. Fortunately, the Grade A listed railway station, one of the finest railway buildings in the United Kingdom, was not affected.

Weymouth Harbour

Opened in 1840 and extended to 900 feet in 1860, a regular steamer service to the Channel Islands was commenced from Weymouth's steamer pier in 1867. A railway, known as the Weymouth Harbour Tramway, was laid in 1865 by the Great Western Railway from Weymouth station to the pier quay, running along Commercial Road and alongside the River Wey. Originally horse-drawn, the line was upgraded for use by steam locomotives in 1880, and on 3 August 1889 passenger trains began using it following the takeover of the Channel Islands steamer services by the GWR. The line was extended onto the pier, which gained a new landing stage and baggage handling hall. On 21 December 1908, the Pavilion Theatre was opened on reclaimed land opposite the pier, which was now 1,050 feet in length. These two postcard views show Weymouth Harbour station *c*. 1910.

Weymouth Harbour

Between 1931 and 1933 Weymouth Pier was entirely rebuilt in concrete to take two full-length rail tracks and new berthing facilities. All of the structural work and maintenance of the pier was the responsibility of Weymouth Corporation, although the Great Western Railway maintained the permanent way and track. On 13 July 1933, the new pier was officially opened by HRH the Prince of Wales and it now measured 1,300 feet in length (above). However, the Pavilion Theatre was burnt down on 13 April 1954, although a new pavilion arose from the ashes and was opened on 14 July 1960. By 1980, work to enlarge the pier had been completed, but regular passenger services on the Weymouth Harbour Tramway (below, in 1976) ceased in 1987 and the last special train ran in May 1999. The line was partially removed in 2020–21. A short-lived miniature railway may have run on the pier in the late 1940s.

Above: **Pier Stations not on Piers: Avonmouth (BPR&P)**
The terminus of the Bristol Port Railway & Pier Company at Avonmouth, opened on 10 April 1865, served a short-lived steamer pier that was beset by a silting up of the water channel. Sailings from the pier had ceased by 1871 and it was quickly demolished. No image of the pier has been found and this is the only one known of the station, which closed on 18 May 1903 to make way for a dock extension.

Below: **Pier Stations not on Piers: Gravesend West Street**
Gravesend West Street station on the London, Chatham & Dover Railway served a pier used by boat services to Holland and by steamers from London to Kent and Essex. Opened on 10 May 1886, the station was closed to passengers on 3 August 1953 and goods on 25 March 1968. Steamer services to the pier ceased in September 1966, but the stout cast-iron structure can still be seen.

Above: **Pier Stations not on Piers: Gravesend Town**

Gravesend Town Pier, pictured in 1895 when the Town Square flooded, was counted as a station by the London, Tilbury & Southend Railway, although it never received a train. The trains terminated at Tilbury on the Essex side of the Thames Estuary, and the two piers were connected by a ferry until 30 March 2024. The pier dates back to 1834 and is the oldest surviving cast-iron pier in the world.

Below: **Pier Stations not on Piers: Tilbury**

The London, Tilbury & Southend Railway's station and pier at Tilbury is pictured below in *c.* 1910. The station and pier were opened in 1855 and were greatly rebuilt in 1906, and again in 1928–30 when a new 1,142-foot-long and 80-foot-wide structure was used as London's Ocean Passenger Terminal, except for the eastern 300 feet exclusively used by the Gravesend Ferry. The station was closed in November 1992.

Above: **Pier Stations not on Piers: Mumbles**
Mumbles Pier station *c.* 1910 on the famous Swansea & Mumbles Railway in South Wales. The railway opened as long ago as 1807 using horse power for the world's first regular railway passenger service. Steam locomotives were introduced in 1877, which were replaced by large electric double-deck cars built by Brush Electric Engineering. The line closed in 1960, but the pier, opened in 1898, is still extant.

Below: **Pier Stations not on Piers: Tollesbury**
Tollesbury Pier station on the Kelvedon & Tollesbury Light Railway was opened on 15 May 1907 and served a 1,770-foot pier, which proved to be a failure as a yachting centre. This led to the pier station being closed to regular traffic from July 1921, although the pier survived until the 1950s. The Kelvedon & Tollesbury Light Railway had opened on 1 October 1904 and closed to passengers in 1951 and goods in 1962.

British Rail 2nd
DAY RETURN
GLASGOW CENTRAL to ARDROSSAN WINTON PIER
Issued subject to conditions
2016
2nd - OFF PEAK RETURN
Balloch (Pier) to GLASGOW (QUEEN ST.)
OFF PEAK - 2nd RETURN
Glasgow (Queen St) to BALLOCH (PIER)
For conditions see over
1931
2nd-SINGLE-EXCHANGE TICKET
Cardiff General to BARRY PIER
via Cogan or Lavernock
Supplementary Charge......
For conditions see over
3348
L.M.S.R. Sailing ticket for Steamer leaving DUN LAOGHAIRE(KINGSTOWN P'R) at 8.30 p.m.
22ND. AUG. 1948
THE PASSENGER MUST ALSO BE IN POSSESSION OF THE USUAL TRAVEL TICKET
SEE OVER
903
L.M.&S.R. FOR CONDITIONS SEE BACK
FIRST CLASS SINGLE
FAIRLIE TO
FAIRLIE PIER
Rly.
Via
FARE......S......D
286
The Locomotive Club of Great Britain
LA CÔTE DU NORD RAIL TOUR
SUNDAY 19th MAY 1968
VICTORIA TO FOLKESTONE HARBOUR & RETURN
For conditions see over
0334
2nd - SINGLE
SINGLE - 2nd
Aberdeen to Aberdeen
GREENOCK (PRINCES PIER)
FARE 32/4
0101
HERNE BAY COUNCIL
PIER TRAMWAY
RETURN FARE 3d
Williamson, Ticket Printer, Ashton
21745
HYTHE PIER
ELECTRIC RAILWAY
This ticket must be given up to the Conductor on demand and does not include Pier Toll
SINGLE Not Transferable
1½P
96116
ONE DOG
Ambleside Pier TO BOWNESS PIER
Bowness Pier TO AMBLESIDE PIER
Rate 0/9
For conditions see over
3405
SINGLE
Lymington Pier to
Lymington Pier Yarmouth Slipway
YARMOUTH SLIPWAY
Including Pier Tolls
For conditions see over
5165
L. & N. E. Railway.
Excess Paid 3d.
NEW HOLLAND.
PIER to STATION OR STATION to PIER
THIRD CLASS.
ON DATE OF ISSUE ONLY.
A 0753
ISLE OF MAN HARBOURS
QUEENS PIER TRAM
ADULT
50844
BRITISH RAILWAYS (S)
RYDE PIER TRAMWAY
NOT TRANSFERABLE.
SINGLE JOURNEY
Fare 2d.
AVAILABLE ONLY FOR ONE JOURNEY IN EITHER DIRECTION.
Ryde Pier Head to Ryde Pier Gates
Ryde Pier Gates to Ryde Pier Head
84 3463
BRITISH RAILWAYS (S)
RYDE PIER
ADMIT ONE CHILD (under 14 years of age)
1½D
FOR CONDITIONS SEE BACK
02328
SOUTHEND-ON-SEA CORPORATION
PIER RAILWAY
CHILD
3D
MONTHLY SEASON TICKET HOLDERS ONLY
NOT TRANSFERABLE
PUNCH & TICKET CO. LONDON, N1
01049
No 1(84040/2)
1st- EXCHANGE TICKET
Stranraer (Harbour) to LARNE (HARBOUR)
The holder is requested to destroy this ticket on completion of journey
(H) For conditions see over
1167
WALTON PIER, LTD. TRAMWAYS.
Adult Fare 2D
SINGLE JOURNEY
PUNCH & TICKET CO. LONDON, N1
J 6737

Above: **Morecambe Stone Jetty**
The Morecambe Stone Jetty in Lancashire was built in 1848 and five years later the North Western Railway extended its line on to the jetty, which was used both for passenger and goods traffic. In 1904, upon the opening of Heysham Harbour, the jetty was used by ship breakers Thomas Ward before it was acquired in 1932 by Morecambe Council, who transformed it into a valuable leisure asset for the town.

Below: **Ballyvoy, Fairhead**
The iron Ballyvoy Pier at Fairhead served the Ballycastle coalfield in County Antrim and was built by the Scottish firm of Merry and Cunningham in 1860 for the North of Ireland Iron and Mining Company. The coalfield went into decline, and the pier was described as derelict in 1922. This photograph, dating from the 1880s–90s, shows coal wagons on the pier and the coal being lowered into a collier by means of a chute.